THE LIFE OF
GEORGE WASHINGTON CARVER

Inventor and Scientist

Series Consultant:
Dr. Russell L. Adams, Chairman
Department of Afro-American Studies, Howard University

Barbara Kramer

Enslow Publishers, Inc.
40 Industrial Road
Box 398
Berkeley Heights, NJ 07922
USA
http://www.enslow.com

Originally published as *George Washington Carver: Scientist and Inventor* in 2002.

Library of Congress Cataloging-in-Publication Data

Kramer, Barbara, author.
  The life of George Washington Carver: inventor and scientist / Barbara Kramer
      pages cm. — (Legendary african americans)
  Includes bibliographical references and index.
  Audience: Grade 4 to 6
  ISBN 978-0-7660-6270-2
  1. Carver, George Washington, 1864?-1943—Juvenile literature. 2. African American agriculturists—
Biography—Juvenile literature. 3. Agriculturists —United States—Biography—Juvenile literature.
4. African Americans—Biography—Juvenile literature. I. Title.
  S417.C3 K73 2015
  630.92—dc23
  [B]
                                        2014027438

Future editions:
Paperback ISBN: 978-0-7660-6271-9
EPUB ISBN: 978-0-7660-6272-6
Single-User PDF ISBN: 978-0-7660-6273-3
Multi-User PDF ISBN: 978-0-7660-6274-0

Printed in the United States of America
102014 Bang Printing, Brainerd, Minn.
10 9 8 7 6 5 4 3 2 1

To Our Readers:
We have done our best to make sure all Internet Addresses in this book were active and appropriate when we
went to press. However, the author and the publisher have no control over and assume no liability for the
material available on those Internet sites or on other Web sites they may link to. Any comments or
suggestions can be sent by e-mail to comments@enslow.com or to the address on the back cover.

♻ Enslow Publishers, Inc., is committed to printing our books on recycled paper. The paper in every
book contains 10% to 30% post-consumer waste (PCW). The cover board on the outside of each book
contains 100% PCW. Our goal is to do our part to help young people and the environment too!

Recipes reprinted by permission of Tuskegee University Archives.

Illustration Credits: Frances Benjamin, 1864–1952, photographer, Johnston/Library of Congress, p. 4.

Cover Illustration: Library of Congress

CONTENTS

This photographic portrait of George Washington Carver was taken by Frances Benjamin Johnston at the Tuskegee Institute in Tuskegee, Alabama.

Chapter 1

"THE PEANUT MAN"

It was a wintry January day in Washington, D.C., in 1921. George Washington Carver waited patiently to address the members of the Ways and Means Committee of the House of Representatives. After two days of hearings, the congressmen were obviously tired and cranky. They were looking forward to the end of a long day when it came time for Carver to speak at 5:00 P.M.

The representatives were considering a tariff bill that would put a tax on agricultural products imported from other countries. The bill was meant to protect growers in the United States who were being hurt by lower-priced imports. Carver had traveled all the way from Tuskegee, Alabama, to talk about the importance of the peanut on behalf of the United Peanut Associations of America.

"When they called my name they were expecting a white man and that created a little confusion," Carver recalled.[1]

The congressmen talked back and forth to one another as Carver made his way to the front of the room. He was fifty-six years old and his hair had started to turn gray. He was tall and thin and his shoulders were stooped as he trudged toward the speaker's stand. He carried a wooden box filled with samples that he intended to show.

"By the time they [the congressmen] were quiet again, I had my samples all ready," Carver recalled.[2]

"All right, Mr. Carver. We will give you ten minutes," the chairman announced.[3]

It was not enough time to even begin all that Carver wanted to say. He had spent years studying the peanut and products that could be made from it. Now he was being asked to talk about his discoveries in only ten minutes, but he did not complain. One by one, he began showing his samples. He spoke in a surprisingly high-pitched voice. This was possibly the result of damage to his vocal cords from a childhood illness. But he was an experienced speaker, and he knew how to hold the attention of his audience.

"Here is a breakfast food. I am very sorry that you can not taste this, so I will taste it for you," he said.[4] His joke brought laughter from the congressmen, who began to relax and show an interest in what the gentleman from Alabama had to say.

The breakfast food was made from a combination of sweet potatoes and peanuts. Carver told the committee that if all other foods were destroyed, people could live on those two products. "From the sweet potato we get starches and carbohydrates, and from the peanut we get all the muscle-building properties," he explained.[5]

When Carver's ten minutes were up, the congressmen asked him to continue. He did, and for more than an hour, he held them spellbound. John N. Garner, a representative from Texas who later became vice president of the United States, called it "a most wonderful exhibition."[6]

Carver displayed other products he had made from the peanut, including milk, fruit drinks, instant coffee, salad oil, and a powder for making ice cream. He had also developed nonfood items such as face cream and ink. Carver, who did not believe in waste, used every part of the peanut. He made insulating board from the shells, and dye from the fine red skin of the peanut. "About thirty different dyes can be made from the skins, ranging from black to orange yellow," he told the congressmen.[7]

On May 27, 1921, Congress passed a protective tariff that placed duties, or taxes, on all agricultural imports. It is impossible to know how much Carver's presentation had to do with the passage of that bill and the fact that peanuts were included in it. But his appearance before the House Ways and Means Committee brought national attention to Carver and his work.

Carver eventually created more than three hundred products from peanuts, earning him a nickname: "The Peanut Man."[8] That was only a small part of the many contributions he made in a long career as a scientist and inventor. Through his work, he quietly changed the lives of thousands of southern farmers, and his discoveries were recognized throughout the world. He was also a well-respected teacher and a fine artist. Those were amazing achievements for any man, but especially for one who began life as a slave in a small southern town.

Chapter 2

"THE PLANT DOCTOR"

George Washington Carver's story began on the Moses Carver farm near Diamond, Missouri. Moses Carver and his wife, Susan, were German immigrants who had settled in the Diamond area about 1838. The Carvers never had children of their own, but when Moses Carver's brother died in 1839, they took in his three children and raised them.

The Carvers did not believe in slavery. With the help of their two nephews and their niece, they were able to run the farm on their own. However, by 1855 the Carvers were middle-aged and the children were grown and living their own lives. The farm was too much for the couple to handle alone. Moses Carver hired a man to help with the farmwork. In spite of his feelings against slavery, he also purchased thirteen-year-old Mary for $700.

The Carvers did not treat Mary like a slave. She was more of a companion to Susan Carver. The two women worked together in the house and garden. Mary lived in a small cabin near the Carver's cabin. On October 10, 1859, Mary had a son, Jim. Although birth records were not normally kept on slaves, Moses Carver recorded Jim's birth.

A few years later, George was born, though the date of his birth is not certain. Considering events early in Carver's life, it is likely that he was born near the end of the Civil War. Many historians have established 1864 as the year of his birth. It is believed that Jim and George had different fathers, but little is known about either man. George was told that his father was the slave of a nearby farmer and that he was killed in a lumbering accident about the time of George's birth.

During the Civil War, Missouri was the site of several bloody battles. At that time, the United States was divided between the North and the South. The North was made up of the Union states—those against slavery. The South was the Confederate states, which approved of slavery. Missouri was a Union state, but many Confederate supporters lived within its boundaries. At different times, both Union and Confederate armies occupied Neosho, a town about eight miles south of Diamond. Residents in the area were victims of looting and killing by both Confederate bushwhackers and Union raiders.

As a Union supporter and a slave owner, Moses Carver was a target for both groups. He was a victim of attacks at least three times during the war. Shortly before the end of the war, a band of men rode onto his farm during the night. Moses Carver was able to hide Jim, but there was no time to warn Mary. The men kidnapped Mary and her baby, George, and took them into Arkansas.

Moses Carver hired John Bentley, a Union scout stationed in Neosho, to find them. Bentley returned with only George, who was seriously ill with whooping cough. Carver paid Bentley for his work by giving him a racehorse valued at $300.

No one knew what happened to Mary. Some people reported that they had seen her headed north. Other people said that she had been sent down the river to Louisiana to be sold. Still others said that she had been killed. Whatever her fate, George never saw his mother again, and he never learned much about her. Susan Carver missed Mary so much that every time George asked her what his mother was like, she began to cry. She could never bring herself to talk about Mary.

The Carvers moved George and Jim into the main cabin and raised them as if the boys were their own children. On December 6, 1865, the Thirteenth Amendment to the Constitution went into effect. This amendment granted freedom to slaves in the United States. George was too young to understand what that meant, and nothing changed for him and his brother. They remained on the Carver farm.

The Carvers got almost everything they needed from the farm. They grew corn, oats, wheat, and potatoes. Their livestock included sheep, cows, hogs, and oxen. They spun fabric for their clothes from flax and hemp, which grew on the farm. They also spun wool from their sheep to use in making warmer clothing. Apples, peaches, pears, and blackberries were laid out to dry in the sun. Then they were stored away for the winter months. Meat was kept in the smokehouse.

In addition to farming, Moses Carver was a beekeeper with more than fifty beehives. He also raised and trained racehorses and raised bloodhounds for foxhunting. George sometimes got himself in trouble by chasing the dogs or getting them to chase him. The dogs barked, creating a terrible racket. Each time, Moses Carver quickly put an end to the commotion and scolded George for stirring up the dogs.

George helped Susan Carver plant and weed the gardens. He also picked fruit, milked cows, sheared sheep, and gathered eggs. But he was a sickly child. He often suffered from respiratory illnesses, which sometimes caused him to lose his voice. He was also small for his age, probably because of his poor health. The Carvers did not require him to do the heavier farmwork. When Jim was old enough, he helped Moses Carver with the fieldwork, while George worked with Susan Carver in the house doing laundry, cleaning, and cooking.

George, who spoke with a stutter when he was in a hurry, was always asking questions. He liked learning to do new things, and he easily picked up skills just by observing others at work. One day after watching Mrs. Carver knit, he decided that he wanted to try it. He made knitting needles by stripping down turkey feathers, and he unraveled an old sock to use for yarn. Then he sat down and taught himself how to knit. He also mastered other crafts such as crocheting, weaving, and quilting. He learned how to spin wool and how to tan hides and make shoes. He also made candles and soap.

For fun, George and Jim liked to go fishing or swimming. They also spent time playing games such as marbles. There were no other African-American children in the area, and they played freely with white children in the community.

Diamond, sometimes called Diamond Grove, got its name from a grove of trees in the shape of a diamond. The town had a general store and a blacksmith shop, which also contained the post office. Another building served as a church on Sundays and the Locust Grove School during the week.

Moses Carver believed in God, but he did not believe in organized religion. He and Susan Carver did not attend church, which could have made them outcasts in the community. At that time, the church was the center of most social events. But the Carvers were well respected in the community, and they were never left out of the fun. Entertainment included activities such as husking bees, quilting bees, apple parings, and logrollings. Moses Carver's fiddle playing was an important part of these gatherings.

Although Moses Carver did not go to church, he allowed George and Jim to attend Sunday school classes. George, who enjoyed singing hymns with the other children, attended Sunday school regularly. But when Moses Carver tried to enroll the boys in the Locust Grove School, which was held in the same building, members of the community objected. The boys were turned away because they were black.

Before the Civil War, there had been laws against teaching slaves to read and write. Slave owners believed that literacy would give slaves power. After the war, when African Americans won their freedom, they also gained the right to an education.

According to the new Missouri Constitution, townships were required to provide a school for black children if there were at least twenty of school age. There were not that many in the Diamond area. Black children could be allowed to attend white schools, but they could also be refused. For George, not being allowed to go to the Locust Grove School was an early lesson in racial prejudice.

To satisfy his desire for knowledge, George explored the woods near the Carver home, learning about plants, insects, and animals. "I literally lived in the woods," he later wrote. "I wanted to know every strange stone, flower, insect, bird, or beast."[1]

George had a talent for nursing sick plants back to health, which earned him the nickname "the Plant Doctor."[2] Friends and neighbors brought George their sickly, wilted plants and he would tell them what to do. He took plants in the worst condition to his secret garden deep in the woods. There he tended to them until they flourished again, later returning them to their owners. Carver noted that he kept his garden secret because he had planted flowers there and "it was considered foolishness in that neighborhood to waste time on flowers."[3]

He was just as interested in rocks, which he collected and kept in a pile by the chimney. Now and then when Moses Carver thought the collection was getting too large, he asked George to get rid of the rocks. "I obeyed but picked up the choicest ones and hid them in another place," George recalled.[4]

Before long, George had built up another collection of rocks in the corner by the chimney. Once again he was asked to move them.

George also brought home live specimens, including frogs and insects, that he stashed in the cabin. After a few encounters with George's specimens, Susan Carver made a new rule: George had to empty his pockets before he entered the house.

The Carvers' neighbors lived in a stately brick house. They allowed George to visit in their kitchen, but one day he boldly wandered into their parlor. There he saw family portraits hanging on the wall. It was the first time he had seen paintings, and they made a big impression on him. "Made by hand— made by hand," George kept repeating to himself.[5] He decided that it was something he wanted to learn and began drawing on anything he could find. He used berries, bark, and roots to add color to his drawings.

George learned to read from a copy of Webster's Elementary Spelling Book. Later, Moses Carver hired the local schoolteacher to tutor him. But it was not enough to satisfy George's thirst for learning. When he was about twelve years old, George went off on his own to school in Neosho, Missouri. He later said that the Carvers permitted him to go because they wanted him to be able to get an education just like white children.

He walked the eight miles to Neosho, and because he arrived after dark, he took refuge in a barn for the night. It turned out to be a wise choice. The barn belonged to Andrew and Mariah Watkins, an African-American couple with no children of their own. They took George into their home. It was the first time that George lived and worked in an African-American environment.

Andrew Watkins worked at odd jobs around town. Mariah Watkins was a laundry woman and a midwife. As a midwife, she sometimes traveled many miles to help a woman having a baby. While she was gone, George took over her duties, cooking and keeping house for Andrew Watkins. People also came to Mariah Watkins for medical help, and she taught George about the plants and herbs she gathered to use as medicine. George helped her with the laundry, and he also did work for other families to earn extra money.

The Watkinses' home was next to the school. Each day, George joined about seventy other African-American children who crowded into the small one-room school. Calvin Jefferson, one of George's classmates, recalled that George never played with the other children at recess. Instead, he spent that time helping Mariah Watkins wash clothes. He propped a schoolbook up in front of him so that he could study his lessons while he worked. "When the bell would ring for school to take up, George would hop over the fence and return to his classes," Jefferson recalled.[6]

George's brother, Jim, joined him in Neosho for a while and attended school there. However, Jim did not have George's enthusiasm for learning. He left school and trained in the plastering trade.

George attended the African Methodist Church with Andrew and Mariah Watkins. Mariah Watkins gave George a Bible, and he began reading it and memorizing passages. Years later, as an adult, Carver was still reading from that same Bible. He still kept his place with a bookmark that he had embroidered with the help of Mariah Watkins.

On December 22, 1878, George earned a certificate of merit from the school, but he was not finished with his education. He heard about a family in town that was moving to Fort Scott, Kansas, about seventy-five miles from Neosho. George decided to continue his education there. He traveled with the family, walking most of the way because the wagon was heavily loaded with the family's belongings.

As soon as George arrived in Fort Scott, he began looking for work. He applied for a job with the Payne family. Mrs. Payne wanted someone who could cook, and she noted that her husband liked his meals prepared in a certain way. George knew how to cook, but he had never heard of the dishes she named that her husband liked. But George was a quick learner, and he was clever. He told Mrs. Payne that he could do the job. Then he said that because he wanted to prepare the meals just right, perhaps she could show him how. In that way, he was able to learn, and his lack of experience never showed. He also became an expert at baking bread and won several prizes in a baking contest.

Although George attended a white school in Fort Scott, there was much racial prejudice in the area. One night he witnessed a scene he would never forget.

Chapter 3

IN SEARCH OF AN
EDUCATION

G eorge was running an errand the night of March 26, 1879, when he saw an angry mob pull a black prisoner from the Fort Scott jail. They beat the prisoner to death, then dragged the body to the public square and set it on fire. George had never seen such a display of racism, and the stench of burning flesh stayed with him long after that terrible night. Years later, as an adult, he wrote, "As young as I was, the horror haunted me and does even now."[1] Fearing for his own life, he left town that night.

He traveled to Olathe, Kansas, where he got a job keeping house for an African-American couple, Ben and Lucy Seymour. The Seymours, like the Watkinses, were childless and they treated George like a son. A few months later, the Seymours moved to Minneapolis, Kansas. George finished the school year and then joined them there in 1880.

In Minneapolis, he lived with the Seymours and opened his own laundry business. He also worked for Dr. J. McHenry. "Carver cared for my father's horses and would frequently drive him around the countryside, carrying his medicine chest as he visited his patients," McHenry's daughter recalled.[2] McHenry also lent Carver books to read.

Carver enrolled at a mostly white high school. He was older than his classmates, but he was well liked. For fun, he took part in school plays. He also taught himself to play the accordion.

There was another George Carver in town, and there were often mix-ups with their mail. To avoid further confusion, George decided to add the middle initial W to his name. When someone asked him what the W stood for, he said, "Washington." However, he personally never used Washington as part of his name. He went by the name George W. Carver.

In the summer of 1883, Carver returned to Diamond, Missouri, to visit Susan and Moses Carver and his brother, Jim. During the following school year, George received news that his brother had died of smallpox. Jim Carver had been working as a plasterer in Seneca, Missouri, when a smallpox epidemic swept through the town. It was a sad time for George Carver, who was now left without any family. "Being conscious as never before that I was left alone, I trusted God and pushed ahead," he recalled.[3]

Carver ended his high school studies in 1884, although it is not certain that he fulfilled the requirements to receive a diploma. "I nearly finished my high school work," he later wrote.[4]

He moved to Kansas City, where he took courses in shorthand and typing. He had planned to work in the Union Telegraph Office but decided to further his education instead. In 1885 he was accepted at Highland College in Highland, Kansas.

That fall, Carver arrived on campus to begin his studies. He had applied to the school by mail, and when college officials saw that he was black, they refused to let him register. It was a big disappointment for Carver.[5] It appeared that he would never achieve his dream of getting a college education. He wanted to leave town right away, but that was not possible. He had spent all his money getting there. He had to stay and work until he had saved up enough to move on.

Carver was hired to do laundry, cleaning, and cooking for a family named Beeler. One of the Beelers' sons had settled in Ness County, Kansas, located near the Colorado border. He had opened a store there, and the town that grew up around it was called Beeler. Carver decided to move to Beeler, where he took a job working for a farmer.

Many settlers were traveling west at the time, lured by promises of free land. In May 1862, Congress had passed the Homestead Act. This program made it possible for settlers to acquire lots of one hundred sixty acres by living on the land for five years and making improvements. Some settlers did not want to wait that long to own their own place. Another option, which began with an earlier program, allowed them to buy the land for $1.25 per acre after only six months. Carver took advantage of that program. On October 20, 1886, he filed an application for his own homestead about two miles south of Beeler.

During that first winter, Carver continued working and living with the farmer. The following year, he built his house. There were no large forests in the area, which meant that wood for housing was not plentiful. Like other homesteaders, Carver built a sod house. He cut grassy pieces of sod and stacked them one on another, like building a house with bricks. When the walls were finished, he made a frame for the roof and then piled sod on top of the frame.

There was one difference between his home and the homes of his neighbors. Along the south side of his house, Carver built an extra room with large windows. This was his conservatory, where he kept a collection of plants native to the area. E. C. Ford was about fourteen or fifteen years old when he visited Carver's home. Ford was spending time with his grandparents, who were Carver's neighbors. They told him about the conservatory and said that he should see it. "When I told him [Carver] why I had come, he took me into this room and I saw that in the windows he had several shelves and on the shelves he had tin cans with various plants that he had brought in from the prairie. The tin cans were in good order and were nicely decorated with colored paper," Ford recalled.[6] Carver also showed Ford his collection of mineral and rock samples.

The only farm implements Carver owned were a spade, a hoe, and a corn planter. He kept a team of horses in a sod barn. He raised corn and had a vegetable garden. He also planted fruit trees, including mulberries, plums, and apricots.

Beeler was primarily a white community, but Carver fit in well. He played his accordion at dances and joined a local literary society. The members met weekly and put on plays, musicals, and debates. Carver was elected editor for the group. He also received his first formal art training from a neighbor, an African-American woman who had previously taught at Talladega College in Alabama.

Homesteading was not an easy life. There were long summer droughts and blizzards in the winter. In 1888, a blizzard in the area killed more than two hundred people. Carver decided that the harsh conditions were not for him. In 1889, he left his homestead, later selling it for $300. He headed east, eventually wandering to Winterset, Iowa.

In Winterset, Carver got a job as head cook at the Schultz Hotel. It was a temporary position. The owner's son was leaving on a musical tour. It was understood that when the son returned, he would take back his old job. When that time came, Carver began his own laundry service.

Carver met Dr. and Mrs. John Milholland when he attended a church service in Winterset, and they became good friends. He and Mrs. Milholland shared interests in flowers, music, and art. Carver taught Mrs. Milholland how to paint, and she gave him singing lessons.

The Milhollands encouraged Carver to continue his education, telling him about Simpson College in Indianola, Iowa. The college was named after Matthew Simpson, a Methodist minister. Simpson had been a friend of Abraham Lincoln's and shared Lincoln's beliefs in equality for all people. The school had already had one African-American student, and the Milhollands knew that Carver would not be turned away because of race.

Carver walked the twenty-five miles to Indianola. One teacher later described his arrival on campus in the fall of 1890: "He came with a satchel full of poverty, a gangling six-foot body, a squeaky falsetto voice, a humble heart and a burning zeal to know everything."[7]

After paying his twelve dollars for tuition, Carver had only fifteen cents left. He spent ten cents on cornmeal and five cents on beef suet. That was all he had to live on the first week. "Modesty prevented me telling my condition to strangers," he explained.[8]

He bought a tub and a washboard on credit from a local merchant and set up a laundry service in an old shack near the campus. The shack also served as his living quarters. An announcement was made at a student assembly about his service, and he soon had all the business he could handle.

Carver quickly made friends with the other students on campus. When they brought him their laundry, they stayed to talk. "He had no furniture so we sat on boxes the merchants in town had permitted him to take," one student recalled.[9]

The students put their money together and bought Carver a table and three chairs. They knew that Carver would not accept their gift, so they delivered it when he was not at home. Because Carver did not know where the furniture came from, he was not able to return it. From time to time, students left other anonymous donations. They slipped tickets to lectures, concerts, and other performances under Carver's door.

Carver also became friends with W. A. Liston and his wife, Sophia. They owned the local bookstore. Carver spent many hours studying in the large bay window on the south side of the Liston home, or under a walnut tree in their yard. Mrs. Liston introduced him to people in the community. In return for all the Listons did for him, Carver landscaped their yard and did other chores for the family.

Carver had enrolled at Simpson College to study art and music. The art studio occupied the whole top floor of the Scientific and Normal Hall. It was a new building, completed in 1889. The high-pitched roof had a huge skylight that filled the room with natural light. The expansive, bright space was perfect for the art students.

Carver had been accepted at the college as a special student, probably because he had not completed his high school requirements. However, his art teacher, Miss Etta Budd, was more concerned about how Carver would fit in with the all-female art department. Carver soon proved that he was well prepared for college-level courses and that he was a talented artist. In fact, he was able to pay for his music courses with his paintings. He studied both vocal music and piano.

In spite of his talent, Miss Budd was concerned about Carver's future. She knew that it would be hard for an African-American man to make a living as an artist. Most of Carver's paintings were of flowers, and knowing his love of nature, she encouraged Carver to study agriculture.

It was a hard decision for Carver to choose between art and agriculture. He loved art, but he also had a desire to help other African Americans. He believed that he could do that better through agriculture. As slaves, African Americans had worked the land for plantation owners. Now they could use that agricultural experience to improve their own lives. Agriculture as a subject for education was a recent development. After the Civil War, farmers became interested in learning about things such as how to improve the soil for better production.

Etta Budd's father was a professor of horticulture, the study of flowers, fruits, and vegetables. He taught at the Iowa State College of Agriculture and Mechanical Arts, now called Iowa State University, in Ames. The college was a leader in the new field of agricultural research, and in August 1891, Carver began his studies there.

Chapter 4

"CAST DOWN YOUR BUCKET WHERE YOU ARE"

C arver was the first African-American student at Iowa State College, and it was not an easy adjustment. His first problem was finding a place to live. As an African American, he was not allowed to stay in the dormitories. That problem was solved by two of Carver's professors. They arranged for him to stay in what had been an office in the horticulture building. In return for the use of the room, Carver served as janitor of the building.

Carver was also not allowed to eat in the dining hall with the rest of the students. Instead, he was required to eat in the basement with African-American workers on campus. Etta Budd heard about that situation and told Carver's friend Mrs. Liston, who decided to do something about it. She visited Carver, touring the campus with him and meeting his instructors. When it came time to eat, she insisted on eating in the basement with Carver. Before she left campus that day, she made it known to school officials that she planned to make other visits. After that, Carver was told to eat in the dining room with the other students.

In spite of that difficult beginning, Carver quickly made friends and eagerly took part in college activities. He joined a debate club known as the Welch Eclectic Society. Because of his knowledge of flowers and art, he was often put in charge of decorating for the society's banquets. He was the football team's first athletic trainer, and many players benefited from his massage abilities. He also joined the college militia, which prepared students to serve with the Iowa National Guard if called into action by the governor. Carver eventually made the rank of captain, the highest rank students could achieve.

What many students later remembered most about Carver was that he always wore a flower in his lapel, a symbol of his love of nature. If a flower was not available, he would wear a flowering weed, a sprig of evergreen, or even a small twig.

In addition to being the janitor in the horticulture building, Carver worked at a variety of odd jobs to pay for his education. He waited tables in the dining room, gardened, cut wood, worked in the fields on the college farms, and cleaned houses.

Carver's grades depended on how well he liked the course. "He was human like the rest of us," the school's registrar recalled. "He was very good in subjects that interested him, average in others."[1]

One subject that interested him was chemistry. He liked taking substances apart to find out what they were made of. He did not like mathematics and history, but even in those classes he never received a grade lower than a B.

27

During his winter vacation at Iowa State, he enrolled in an art class at Simpson College. Carver's instructors and the other students at Iowa State, who knew about his interest in art, encouraged him to pursue it more. In 1892, they urged him to enter an art exhibit to be held after Christmas in Cedar Rapids, Iowa. Carver said it would not be possible. He could not afford the train fare, and he did not have a suit to wear.

His friends and professors wanted to help, but they had to find a way that Carver could not refuse their gift. Students put their plan into action the day after Christmas. Carver was scheduled to go to Professor Budd's house to clean up after their holiday activities. Budd lived about a mile from campus, and during the night, a light snow had fallen. A sleigh was sent to pick up Carver. Other students crowded in, saying that they wanted to hitch a ride downtown.

When they got downtown, the sleigh stopped in front of one of the biggest stores in Ames. One young man suggested that they all go inside. Then the students headed for the men's department, telling Carver to come with them. They tried to persuade him to try on a suit, but he protested, saying it would be a waste of time because he could not afford to buy it. The students persisted, and Carver finally gave in. The students added shoes, a hat, a coat, and gloves. When the outfit was complete, they informed Carver that the clothes had already been paid for. Carver was then handed a railroad ticket to Cedar Rapids.

That evening, Carver, dressed in his new clothes and carrying four of his paintings, boarded the train for Cedar Rapids. One of Carver's paintings was selected to be exhibited at the World's Columbian Exposition in Chicago in the summer of 1893. That painting, titled *Yucca Gloriosa*, was of the yucca plant that Carver remembered from his homesteading days in Kansas. "I painted that from my memories of the Western plains," he recalled.[2]

Carver's religious beliefs continued to be an important part of his life. He joined a Sunday school class taught by one of his professors, James G. Wilson. The class was so popular that Wilson had to cut back on the number of students. He decided to "graduate" about twenty-five students. Carver was one of that group of graduated students, and he was not happy about it. "We all left him, sad and reluctantly," Carver recalled. "We gave him to understand, in no uncertain terms, that we did not like it at all, and out of love for him, we went, but in less then two months we were all back again."[3]

He was also active in the Young Men's Christian Association (YMCA). He was chosen to represent that group at the National Students' Summer School at Lake Geneva, Wisconsin, for both 1893 and 1894.

As part of his requirements for graduation, Carver had to write a long report called a thesis. One of his particular interests was crossbreeding plants to create new hybrids. This was new science at the time, and Carver wrote about the process in his thesis, "Plants as Modified by Man." The purpose of crossbreeding was to combine the best qualities of two different plants to create a new, more desirable plant. For example, Carver produced hardier flowers with larger blossoms through crossbreeding. He also created new varieties of plants. In one experiment, he crossed a white geranium with a scarlet geranium to produce a plant with salmon-colored blossoms.

Carver earned his bachelor of science degree in agriculture in 1894. His graduating class called itself the Gourds, and its motto was "Ever Climbing." During the graduation ceremony, Carver read "Ode to the Gourds," a poem he had written for the class.

Carver was offered a job working for a florist, but he turned it down. Instead, he decided to stay on at Iowa State to pursue his master's degree. He was also asked to join the faculty, becoming the first African American on the college's staff. Carver was put in charge of the greenhouse and assigned to teach some freshman biology courses.

Although Carver had many friends on campus, there were still episodes of prejudice even after he began teaching. As an instructor, Carver often ate with students in the cafeteria rather than joining other faculty members. One day, he sat down next to a new student from the South. The student made noise with his silverware and chair, showing that he did not like Carver's sitting there. Then the student got up and moved to another table. The students at that table had seen what happened. To show their support for Carver, they all got up and moved to his table.

Carver was also assigned to work in the bacteriological laboratories under the direction of Dr. Louis H. Pammel. Pammel was a well-known expert on mycology, the study of fungi and plant diseases. Carver joined him in that work and developed a great respect for his teacher. He later wrote that Pammel "influenced my life possibly more than anyone else."[4]

Carver worked with Pammel on two publications about plant diseases. With his artistic abilities, Carver was able to make fine drawings of plants to use in the publications.

Carver spent many hours wandering throughout the area looking for sick plants. When he found one, he would bring it back to the lab. There he would study the fungi that had attacked the plant to figure out how to protect plants from that disease.

Henry A. Wallace, the son of one of Carver's professors, Henry C. Wallace, liked to join Carver on his excursions. They were odd companions, the six-foot African-American man walking alongside the six-year-old white boy. But those walks sparked an early interest in plants for Wallace, who remembered Carver as "the kindliest, most patient teacher I ever knew."[5]

Carver also seemed pleased to explore the area with young Wallace. Perhaps Wallace reminded Carver of what he had been like as a child. "He was such an inquisitive little youngster," Carver recalled. "He wanted to know everything about every plant."[6]

Wallace went on to enjoy a long, successful career in agriculture. He spent many years breeding corn to make better hybrids. He later became U.S. secretary of agriculture under President Franklin D. Roosevelt, serving until 1940. He was then nominated as a candidate for vice president of the United States on Roosevelt's ticket and was inaugurated on January 20, 1941.

Carver's work also included traveling throughout the state giving talks on agriculture. At that time, there was nationwide interest in improving orchards. Carver was employed by the

Horticultural Society of Iowa to crossbreed fruit trees such as apple, pear, and plum. His job was to create hardier varieties of fruits that could survive Iowa's cold winter months.

At the same time, he continued his work as a mycologist. His collection of fungi eventually grew to about twenty thousand specimens. It is likely that Carver could have made great discoveries as a mycologist, but his life soon took a different turn.

In November 1895, he was offered a job as chairman of agriculture at the Alcorn Agricultural and Mechanical College in Westside, Mississippi. Faculty members at Iowa State praised Carver's abilities and recommended him strongly. On the other hand, they also noted how valuable he was to Iowa State. They asked Carver to stay on at his present position.

Carver did not make a decision immediately. He was not scheduled to receive his master's degree until the fall of 1896, so he put the Alcorn job on hold. Then in March 1896, he received a letter from Booker T. Washington. Washington was founder and principal of the Tuskegee Institute, an African-American school in Tuskegee, Alabama.

Like Carver, Washington had been born a slave. He grew up in Malden, West Virginia, where he worked in a salt mine during the day and attended school at night. He furthered his education at the Hampton Institute, an African-American school in Hampton, Virginia. In 1881, he founded the Tuskegee Institute. His focus at the institute was helping African Americans improve their lives by learning practical skills such as carpentry, bricklaying, and farming.

Carver was aware of Washington's work at the institute. He was also familiar with a famous speech that Washington had given in Atlanta, Georgia, on September 18, 1895. Many African Americans were migrating from farmlands to cities. They were hoping to find a better life in the cities, but they often ended up living in slums. In his Atlanta speech, Washington urged African Americans to stay on the farms. "Cast down your bucket where you are," he said.[7]

That phrase came from a story he told about a ship that was lost at sea for many days. When a friendly ship came by, the captain of the lost ship sent a message asking for water. The reply from the other ship was, "Cast down your bucket where you are." Sailors on the lost ship were afraid to drink the water around them, thinking that they were in salt water. It took several messages back and forth before sailors on the lost ship finally cast down their bucket and discovered fresh water. They were in the mouth of the Amazon River.

Rather than moving to other areas, Washington urged African Americans to improve conditions where they were. Carver shared Washington's interest in helping African Americans better their lives. But he hesitated when Washington invited him to join the Tuskegee faculty. In his reply to Washington, Carver noted that he had other offers and that he was still working on his master's degree.

A couple of days later, it appeared that Carver had thought more about the offer. He wrote another letter to Washington indicating that he was interested in the position. Carver believed that he had a mission, a calling from God, to help other African Americans. Being a member of the faculty of the

Tuskegee Institute would give him that opportunity. In a letter to Washington dated April 12, 1896, he wrote, "Of course it has always been the one great ideal of my life to be of the greatest good to the greatest number of 'my people' possible and to this end I have been preparing myself for these many years; feeling as I do that this line of education is the key to unlock the golden door of freedom to our people."[8]

The Tuskegee Institute was adding an agricultural department, and Washington wanted Carver to head it. Washington was committed to having an all-black faculty at the institute. He noted that Carver was the only African American qualified for such a position. If Carver would not accept, Washington would be forced to consider hiring a white instructor.

Washington warned Carver that he would not be able to pay him as much as he might get from other schools. He offered Carver a salary of $1,000 a year plus a place to live in a campus dormitory. Carver accepted the offer, and Washington agreed to hold the position until Carver completed his master's degree in agriculture.

Carver received that degree in October 1896. He was thirty-two years old and ready to begin a new life. He packed everything except his mycological collection, which he donated to Iowa State. The students and teachers at Iowa State presented Carver with a microscope, complete with its own carrying case.

On October 5, 1896, Carver left for Alabama, where a much different environment awaited him.

Chapter 5

SCIENTIFIC AGRICULTURE

A s Carver's train chugged into Alabama, he could not help noticing the signs of extreme poverty. After the Civil War, many former slaves had become tenants. They rented land from white owners. As tenants, they had to plant what the landowners told them to grow. In the South, that meant cotton. After many years of cotton crops, the land was worn out. Tenant farmers grew barely enough cotton to pay their rent. Hoping to make more money, the farmers used every bit of land. They planted cotton right up to the doors of the small, unpainted shacks that were their homes.

There were only thirteen students enrolled in Tuskegee's agricultural program that first semester. Students were not interested in studying agriculture. They saw education as a way to escape the poverty of farming. Carver would have to show them that farmers could make a good living in the South. He started by introducing them to scientific agriculture, using science to find ways to make farming more profitable.

There was no money for a laboratory, so Carver created one, using what was available. He and his students collected jars, bottles, old wire, cans, and other materials from a nearby dump. Carver cut off the tops of bottles to make beakers and used an old gaslight as a Bunsen burner. For his experiments, Carver needed a way to grind substances into a fine power. Usually, this was done by placing them in a mortar and mashing them with a pestle. Carver had neither, so he made do. He found a heavy kitchen cup to use as a mortar. A flat piece of iron became his pestle.

At that time, the government provided funding for experiment stations at colleges and universities. These were plots of land used for farming experiments. The federal government granted money to each state. Then the state legislatures decided where the money was to go. In 1897, the Alabama State Legislature approved funding for an experiment station at the Tuskegee Institute. It was the first all-black experiment station in the United States. Carver was named director.

The soil on the station's sixteen-acre plot was sandy and worn out from too many years of growing cotton. "Everyone told me that the soil was unproductive. But it was the only soil I had," Carver noted.[1] He needed to find a way to make the land produce.

Carver knew that plants required certain things from the soil. After years of growing cotton, the soil no longer had what the plants needed. The first step was to put nutrients back into the soil. One way to do that was by fertilizing. Commercial fertilizer was expensive, so Carver gave his students buckets and sent them into swampy, woodsy areas to gather leaves and other decaying plant matter. They used this natural fertilizer, spreading it on the ground of the experiment station.

Carver also knew that different plants had different needs. Another way to rebuild the soil was to plant crops that would replace the nutrients that cotton took out of the soil. Plants such as cowpeas, velvet beans, and clover were able to take nitrogen from the air and put it into the soil. Cotton needed that nitrogen. Alternating, or rotating, these crops with cotton would replenish the soil between cotton plantings.

Carver was excited about what he taught, and that enthusiasm spread to his students. They also liked his practical, hands-on teaching style. Interest in the agricultural program grew. In Carver's second semester at the institute, there were seventy-five students enrolled in his department.

As a scientist, Carver taught his students that it was important to be exact. He said that about was never right, and he illustrated his point with a story. "If you come to a stream five feet wide and jump four and a half feet, you fall in and get drowned. You might just as well have tumbled in from the other side and saved yourself the exertion of the jump," he explained.[2]

The students were impressed with how much Carver knew about agriculture and nature. They also enjoyed his sense of humor. One day as a joke, a group of his students put together an insect specimen made from parts of different insects. The new specimen had an ant's head, a beetle's body, spider legs, and antennae from a moth. The students pinned the various sections together on a piece of cardboard and then asked Carver to identify it.

Carver studied the strange-looking insect for a while. Then he said, "Well, this, I think, we would call a *hum*bug."[3] (A humbug is a trick or a fraud.)

Carver's reputation as an expert on all kinds of plants quickly spread beyond the campus. Booker T. Washington, who knew Carver as a quiet, almost timid man, wondered how people in the community had found out about Carver's skills.

"You must have some way of advertising," Washington joked.[4]

Carver explained that it had happened almost by accident. He had a habit of starting his day very early with walks through the woods and the countryside. During his walks, he gathered plants, molds, and other specimens. The walks were also a spiritual time. "Alone there with the things I love most, I gather specimens and study the great lessons that Nature is so eager to teach me. In the woods each morning, while most other persons are sleeping, I best hear and understand God's plan for me," he said.[5]

On those walks, he always took his botany can, a cylinder with a lid and a carrying strap, for gathering his specimens. Often, he talked to people he met along the way. Carver was out walking one morning when he met a woman from the community. Seeing his botany can, she wondered if he was a peddler, or salesman. When he explained what he was doing, she asked him to come look at her roses, which were diseased. He showed her what she needed to do to save her roses and even wrote it down for her. "In this," Carver said, "and several other ways, it became noised abroad that there was a man at the school who knew about plants. People began calling upon me for information and advice."[6]

Carver was also known for forming long-lasting friendships. At Tuskegee, he wrote letters to keep in contact with friends he had made while at Simpson College and Iowa State College. One of those friends was his former professor Dr. Louis H. Pammel.

In a letter to Pammel dated March 30, 1897, Carver said that he was happy with his new position. "I am enjoying my work very much indeed," he wrote. "The weather is simply superb, and as for flowers I never saw anything like it. This is indeed a new world to Iowa. Very poor to be sure but many things to make it pleasant. I like it so much better than I thought I would at first."[7]

It appeared that Carver had decided to focus on what he liked about his job in that letter. One thing he did not mention was that other faculty members did not make him feel welcome.

Carver was the only person on the faculty who had earned an advanced degree from a white college. Most of the other staff members had been educated at African-American schools that taught practical trades. Many had attended the Hampton Institute or had graduated right there from the Tuskegee Institute. They resented Carver's high level of education and the fact that he was paid a higher salary than they were.

Carver also got off on the wrong foot when he asked for two rooms for his living quarters. At that time, bachelor instructors were expected to share a room with another faculty member. But Carver had brought books and his many collections with him. How could he be expected to do his work if he did not have a place for his equipment? he wondered. Washington gave Carver only one room, but Carver did not have to share it with another instructor.

Soon after he arrived at Tuskegee, Carver also made it known that he planned to be there only a few years. Then he wanted to return to painting. In a letter to the finance committee, he wrote, "I do not expect to teach many years, but will quit as soon as I can trust my work to others, and engage in my brush work, which will be of great honor to our people showing to what we may attain, along, [sic] science, history, literature and art."[8] Other instructors wondered why Carver should be given special treatment if he intended to be there only a short time.

Not all faculty members felt that way. Carver did form friendships with some other instructors. But much of the time he kept to himself, and he rarely took part in social activities on campus.

Carver also had problems with Booker T. Washington. Washington liked Carver's teaching abilities, but Carver was not a good administrator. This led to many disagreements between the two men. Washington was very organized. He got frustrated with Carver's lack of organization. Washington complained when a report was late, saying that Carver was not paying attention to his administrative work.

For his part, Carver said that he had too much to do. He liked to be able to focus on one thing at a time, a habit he had formed as a student at Iowa State College. "In this work of mine I have my mind fixed on one object and find it. I have the others in mind, but I do not look for them until I am ready," he once explained.[9] Focusing on one thing at a time was not possible at the institute, where Carver's duties went far beyond the classroom.

In addition to teaching and serving as director of the experiment station, he had the work of heading a department. That meant attending meetings and writing reports. He also managed the school's two farms, which supplied food for the Tuskegee staff and students. This included tending to the institute's livestock—dairy cows, chickens, pigs, sheep, and oxen. Since the institute did not yet have a veterinarian, Carver filled that position for a time, too.

He was even in charge of landscaping. During his first winter on campus, Carver came up with a plan for landscaping that looked attractive. When spring came, he put his plan into action. He soon became discouraged, though, because students and faculty members took shortcuts across his newly planted grass. It was impossible to get the grass to grow with everyone walking all over it.

Instead of getting angry with the students and faculty, Carver looked at what he could do differently. He spent a few days watching the paths that they normally took. Then he changed his landscaping to include those natural paths.

Another part of Carver's job was fund-raising for the agricultural program. One year, he toured through several southern states, giving piano concerts to raise money.

Carver was also responsible for organizing and planning the new agricultural building that was being built. In December 1897, that building was dedicated. James G. Wilson, one of Carver's professors at Iowa State, was now U.S. secretary of agriculture under President William McKinley. Carver asked Wilson to show support for the institute by taking part in that dedication. There was much excitement at the institute and in the community as they prepared for Wilson's two-day visit. It was the first time the school had received this kind of national support.

During the summer, when there were no classes, Carver was busy with several outside projects. He worked with the Alabama Polytechnic Institute on a study of fungi in the state. In addition, he teamed up with the Smithsonian Institution to gather data on plants in the United States that could be used in making medicine. He also joined forces with the U.S. Department of Agriculture (USDA) on a project to gather specimens of all the grasses in the United States.

Carver was also involved with an adult education program for area farmers. Booker T. Washington had started this program in 1892 with a farmer's conference held at Tuskegee. By the time Carver arrived on campus, the conference was an annual event held in February. Each year, the night before the conference, farmers and their families began arriving in buggies, wagons, and carts. Others rolled in during the early morning hours, after traveling through the night.

The day began with a parade. Then Washington spoke to the crowd and encouraged farmers to share their accomplishments. At noon they feasted on barbecued oxen, pigs, and sheep that had been prepared by the institute. In the afternoon, the farmers roamed the campus watching various demonstrations. Carver gave demonstrations at the experiment station and led tours through the station's plot. He also handed out packets of free seeds provided by the USDA. In the evening, the farmers and their families began their trip home.

Carver also began holding monthly meetings for area farmers at the institute. At these meetings, he talked about crop rotation, fertilizer, and soil conservation. He encouraged farmers to bring in soil samples. Carver analyzed the samples in his makeshift laboratory. Then he told each farmer how to improve his soil. Farmers also reported on improvements they were making on their farms. When wives started attending the meetings with their husbands, Carver added kitchen demonstrations. Senior girls at the institute prepared these programs for the women.

In 1898, the institute held a fair. Farmers brought livestock and samples of crops. Their wives brought needlework and foods that they had prepared. All of these were displayed in exhibits much like those at today's county fairs. The fair also became an annual event.

Another way that Carver reached out to area farmers was by publishing bulletins. These related to work he was doing at the experiment station. This was not something new. Other experiment stations published their results too. However, Carver's bulletins were different from the scholarly reports put out by other experiment stations.

Carver realized that if he was going to help the people he wanted to help—poor southern farmers with limited education—he needed to present the information in a way that they understood. As a result, the bulletins were written in simple language.

Carver's first bulletin, "Feeding Acorns to Livestock," was published in 1898. He followed that bulletin with another one released later that year, "Experiments with Sweet Potatoes." He encouraged farmers to plant sweet potatoes. One reason was that they grew well in poor ground. Another advantage was that their growing season was short. It was possible to plant two crops of sweet potatoes in one season. They were perishable, but Carver said that drying them in the sun could preserve them. He also noted that the leaves and vines of the sweet potato could be used as feed for pigs.

Carver worked hard to introduce new ideas to southern farmers, but the farmers were slow to change. They were especially reluctant to give up their one-crop system. Raising cotton was their way of life and had been for many years. In 1902, Carver wrote about that situation: "The Southern farmers, as a whole, have been too slow to admit that the old one-crop idea and primitive implements are quite out of harmony with the new up-to-date methods and machinery."[10]

The farmers were not the only ones who needed to make changes. Living in the South meant new adjustments for Carver. One was getting used to the racially charged environment.

Chapter 6

REACHING OUT TO FARMERS AND STUDENTS

In 1896, about the time that Carver arrived in Alabama, the U.S. Supreme Court handed down its *Plessy* v. *Ferguson* decision. That ruling went against a section of the 1875 Civil Rights Act. This act said that there could be no racial discrimination in places such as schools, restaurants, and hotels. The *Plessy* v. *Ferguson* decision said just the opposite. Blacks could be denied entrance to places designated for whites only as long as there were equal facilities for blacks. The state police in Alabama strictly enforced this ruling, even though facilities for blacks were not at all equal to what was available to whites.

Carver had experienced this kind of prejudice before, but he never complained. With his quiet, friendly manner, he often found acceptance among people who had first judged him by the color of his skin. But in November 1902, he got caught in the middle of a racial situation in Ramer, Alabama, that left him shaken.

Carver had traveled to Ramer by train to meet with Nelson E. Henry, an African-American teacher. Frances B. Johnston was also on that train. She was a white photographer traveling throughout the South gathering information on black schools. The train arrived at night, and Henry picked up both Johnston and Carver at the station. People in the community did not like the fact that Johnston was in the buggy with two African American men.

Henry dropped Carver off at a house outside town, where he would spend the night with a black family. Henry had arranged for Johnston to stay overnight with a black family, too. Johnston thought it would be better if she stayed with a white family, so Henry took her back into town. They were met there by three angry young men. The men argued with Henry and then fired shots at him as he escaped on foot into the night.

Johnston went to Carver and told him what had happened. Fearing that the men would be after him, too, Carver quickly left the house where he was staying. He took Johnston to the next station where she could leave on a train in the morning. Carver then spent the rest of the night walking, trying to stay out of the men's reach. "I had the most frightful experience of my life there," he later wrote, "and for one day and night it was a very serious question indeed as to whether I would return to Tuskegee alive or not as the people were thoroughly bent upon bloodshed."[1]

In the meantime, tensions between Carver and Washington grew in 1902 with the hiring of George R. Bridgeforth. Bridgeforth did not like Carver's administration. He made his feelings known by writing letters to both Washington and Carver. In the letters, he criticized Carver's management of the agricultural department. Things came to a head in September 1904, when Bridgeforth complained about Carver's handling of the poultry flock. Washington appointed a committee to look into the situation.

The committee reported that the poultry flock was in bad shape. It also suggested that Carver had submitted false reports to Washington to cover up those problems. Carver was hurt that the committee would suggest that he had not told the truth. In a letter to Washington, he wrote that being called a liar "is more than I can bear."[2]

Bridgeforth had Washington's attention, and he struck again. This time, he asked Washington to take away some of Carver's responsibilities. Washington appointed another committee to look into that possibility. The committee said that the department should be divided between Carver and Bridgeforth. Carver would be director of the experiment station and in charge of agricultural instruction. Bridgeforth would be director of agricultural industries, which included the institute's livestock.

It was a chance for Carver to give up some of his work, but he was not happy with that plan. One reason was that he wanted a chance to solve the problems with the poultry flock.

Another reason was that he believed the change in duties was a step down in his position. He thought there should be one department head with divisions under it.

In November 1904, Carver sent Washington a letter of resignation. He had not taken time to think about that action. When he did, he changed his mind. A few days later, he sent Washington another letter, saying that he would consider staying on at the institute. Washington did not act on the committee's plan, and Carver remained in charge of the agricultural department.

Although the poultry operation was in bad shape, Carver enjoyed success with the experiment station. During his first year at the institute, the station lost $2.50 per acre. The next year it showed a small profit. In 1904 the station had a net gain of $75 per acre. The following year, Carver harvested a five-hundred-pound bale of cotton from one acre of land. That was four times the average output. The increases came from the methods of improving the soil that Carver had talked about since he first arrived at the institute. This included using fertilizer and rotating cotton with other crops.

In 1904, Carver expanded the adult education program, teaching daytime classes for farmers during the winter months. It started as a six-week course, but it was later shortened to two weeks.

Carver shared his knowledge with many farmers through the institute's annual conferences and fairs, monthly meetings, and winter classes, and through his bulletins. However, he realized that he was reaching only the better-informed farmers. He wanted to help the farmers who never even heard about these opportunities. To do that, he needed to travel to them.

In May 1906, Carver started a movable school called the Jesup Wagon. It was named after Morris K. Jesup, a New York banker who partially funded the project. Students at the institute built the wagon. Carver equipped it with plows and other tools to demonstrate better ways of farming. He also added a cream separator, a butter churn, and other equipment of interest to homemakers.

On weekends, Carver and his students loaded up the Jesup Wagon and traveled to area farms to give demonstrations. They arranged in advance to stop at particular farms. Other farmers in the area also came to watch and listen.

The farms that Carver traveled to in Alabama were very different from the Moses Carver farm where he had spent his early years. The Carver farm had provided almost everything the family needed. In Alabama at that time, farms were devoted almost entirely to cotton. The farmers did not have gardens, and only a few had livestock such as pigs, chickens, and cows. The families suffered health problems caused by a poor diet.

During that summer, more than two thousand farmers a month turned out for demonstrations at the Jesup Wagon. Carver encouraged them to plant gardens. He talked to the women about how to preserve and prepare the foods they grew. He taught farmers how to cure meat and how to run a profitable farm. He also talked to farmers about taking pride in their work. Part of that pride would come from ownership. Carver urged farmers to set aside a little money each day so that they could save to buy land.

That fall, the U.S. Department of Agriculture (USDA) took over the Jesup Wagon, appointing Thomas Campbell, a former student of Carver's, to supervise the wagon. Campbell was the USDA's first African-American demonstration agent.

Carver took pride in the accomplishments of his students, and he greatly influenced their lives. They often came to him for personal advice. If they needed money, Carver would help. He preferred that the money be a loan, because he wanted them to be responsible. On the other hand, he sometimes just gave students small amounts of money when they needed it. He helped many of them find good jobs when they graduated. For those who wanted to continue their education, he offered guidance in getting scholarships. He kept in contact with many of his students, corresponding with them long after they had left Tuskegee.

It was not just the students in his classes who benefited from Carver's help. In 1903, Rockefeller Hall, a boys' dormitory, was built. Carver moved into two rooms on the ground floor, finally getting his wish for more space. Young men living in the dorm also came to him for help and advice.

In the spring of 1907, a small group of people gathered in Carver's office to organize a Bible class on campus. They asked Carver to lead it. It gave him an opportunity to influence the lives of even more students. His Bible class was a popular one, and it grew until the average attendance was about two hundred students.

Unfortunately, Carver's problems with Bridgeforth continued. In 1908, Bridgeforth once again complained about Carver's handling of the poultry yard. This time Washington followed through on the plan proposed by the committee four years earlier. Carver became the director of agricultural instruction and the experiment station. Bridgeforth was named director of agricultural industries.

Two years later, Washington took more responsibilities away from Carver. At that time, Carver became director of the newly created Department of Agricultural Research and the director of the experiment station. This meant that Carver would be able to spend more time on research. Washington also promised Carver a new, better-equipped laboratory.

It appeared that Washington was trying to put Carver in charge of the type of work that he did best. On the other hand, Washington would not allow anyone to remain on staff for research only. Everyone was required to teach. Because of the way duties were divided, Carver was forced to teach a few classes under the direction of Bridgeforth.

Carver and Washington continued to disagree. One of Carver's complaints was that the laboratory that Washington promised took too long to actually come together. Although they disagreed, the two men had great respect for each other. They also shared a goal of helping their people. Carver wrote letters of complaint to Washington, but he also wrote letters praising Washington and the work he was doing.

In the meantime, Carver's reputation off campus was growing. He was invited to speak at conferences and fairs in other states, including Mississippi, Georgia, South Carolina,

Florida, and Kentucky. As his work became better known, requests for his bulletins increased. Some came from as far away as South America, Europe, and Australia. Two bulletins that were especially popular were "How to Build Up Worn Out Soils" and "Cotton Growing on Sandy Upland Soils."

In his laboratory, Carver had been working on developing a new cotton hybrid. It would combine the best qualities of short-stalk and tall-stalk cotton. Short-stalk cotton was desirable because it produced the fattest cotton bolls. But the cotton was so close to the ground that it was easily damaged during rainstorms. The rain would splatter the sandy soil onto the cotton bolls. Cotton on tall stalks was at a protected distance from the soil, but the bolls it produced were smaller. In 1910, Carver introduced his new hybrid—a tall plant with fatter cotton bolls. It was officially named Carver's Hybrid.

That year, Carver also published a bulletin titled "Possibilities of the Sweet Potato in Macon County, Alabama." In his laboratory, Carver had been working on finding new uses for the sweet potato. His discoveries included making breakfast foods, tapioca, molasses, coffee, vinegar, caramels, and flour from sweet potatoes. Nonfood products made from sweet potatoes included starch, library paste, ink, shoe polish, and wood fillers.

Carver also experimented with making stains and paints from the clay that was so plentiful in the Alabama soil. Seeing the unpainted homes of the farmers inspired him to come up with an inexpensive paint. "The reason farmers down here don't paint their homes isn't because they are lazy or don't care," he noted. "It is because they don't have cash money to buy paint."[3]

He extracted color from the clay and mixed it with used motor oil to produce paint at very little cost. His bulletin on this process, "White and Color Washing with Native Clays from Macon County, Alabama," was published in 1911.

Carver did not have much time for his art, but he worked on it when he could. In his paintings, he used colors that he created from the Alabama clay. Through his experiments, he was able to produce a blue that had previously been found only in Egyptian tombs in the Nile Valley. A method of making that color paint had become a lost art until Carver rediscovered it.

Carver also created other products from clay. They included talcum powder and a powder for cleaning metals. But it was his work with the peanut that would bring him fame.

Chapter 7

THE BOLL WEEVIL, WAR, AND RACIAL PREJUDICE

―――――――⎯⎯⎯⎯⎯――――――

arver's early interest in the peanut was in finding crops that would replenish the soil. "The peanut crop is profitable because it has power to extract nitrogen from the air and deposit it in the soil, thus becoming a soil builder rather than a soil robber," Carver explained.[1] But farmers were not interested in peanuts. Some had small patches of peanuts that they grew as a treat for children to eat. Other than that, there appeared to be little use for them. Carver said that peanuts could be fed to livestock, but the farmers did not want to grow them for this purpose.

It was an insect that changed their minds. There were reports that the boll weevil was sweeping across Texas. The boll weevil ate cotton plants, and it was wiping out entire fields. By 1910, it had worked its way into Alabama. Carver urged farmers to burn off their cotton fields—a common practice of setting fields on fire to clear the land—and then to plant peanuts. They did as he suggested.

Carver soon realized that he had another problem. One day a widow came to Carver's laboratory wondering what to do. She had more peanuts than her livestock could eat. Other farmers also complained. Their storehouses were full of peanuts, and peanuts were rotting in the fields because there was no place to sell them.

Carver felt that he had created the problem and now he needed to fix it by finding more uses for peanuts. He had already begun experimenting with the peanut as a way to improve the diets of southerners. The peanut was a good source of protein. Meat, a more common source of protein, was too expensive for many people. Peanuts were more affordable.

In his laboratory, Carver broke the peanut down into its various parts. These included amino acids, starches, oils, fats, and proteins. "There! I had the parts of the peanut all spread out before me," Carver said. "Then I merely went on to try different combinations of those parts, under different conditions of temperature, pressure, and so forth."[2]

With this method, Carver created breakfast foods, sauces, beverages, flour, pickles, and candy. He combined hydrogen with peanut oil to produce oleomargarine. Then he broke down the fat globules to produce milk. The milk from peanuts had most of the benefits of regular milk, but it had the advantage of being less perishable. From the cream that rose to the top of the milk, he made butter, buttermilk, and cheeses.

Then Carver came up with an unusual plan to show the diversity of the peanut as a food product. With the help of students from the home economics department, Carver prepared a whole meal from peanuts. He served it to Booker T. Washington and a group of area businessmen. The menu included a soup made from peanuts and a salad of chopped up peanuts and apples. The main course appeared to be chicken, but it was not. It was actually a mixture of mashed peanuts, eggs, and bread crumbs spread over sliced sweet potatoes and then fried. He served creamed peanuts as a vegetable. Dessert was cake using flour made from peanuts, and a beverage that tasted like coffee but was actually an imitation that Carver created from peanuts.

Carver published the results of his work in a bulletin titled "How to Grow the Peanut and 105 Ways of Preparing It for Human Consumption." In addition, he created many nonfood items from peanuts. These included shaving lotion, face powder, ink, axle grease, shampoo, wood filler, and metal polish.

His success in the laboratory was soon overshadowed by sadness. In 1915, Booker T. Washington was on a fund-raising tour when he collapsed in New York. He returned to Tuskegee, where he died on November 14. Carver was so upset by Washington's death that he took several months off from teaching. It appeared that he also had regrets about his past disagreements with Washington. In a letter to one of Washington's friends, Carver wrote, "I am sure Mr. Washington never knew how much I loved him, and the Cause for which he gave his life."[3]

Robert Russa Moton from the Hampton Institute took over Washington's position. Carver had a good working relationship with him. Eventually, Moton was able to relieve Carver of his teaching responsibilities, allowing him more time for research.

Carver's work as a scientist soon brought him an international award. In 1916, he was elected a fellow of England's Royal Society of Arts, Manufacturers and Commerce. He was the first African American to be recognized by that organization. It brought him a great deal of attention as newspaper reporters wrote about the former slave who had become a member of a royal society.

Carver also attracted the attention of the inventor Thomas Edison. Edison was interested in Carver's research into producing rubber from the sweet potato. According to reports, Edison offered Carver a huge salary to work with him for five years in his laboratory in West Orange, New Jersey. Carver said that he could not leave Tuskegee. He recalled how Washington had said, "Cast down your bucket where you are."[4]

"I have done that," Carver noted. "Always it has come up brimful and running over. And there is much more that I want to find out that I can just as well find out here."[5]

In 1917, the United States entered World War I. Production and trade were interrupted during the war, causing a worldwide food shortage. Because of a wheat shortage, the United States government became interested in the flour that Carver had made from sweet potatoes instead of wheat.

In January 1918, Carver was asked to travel to Washington, D.C., to discuss his discoveries. Carver baked some of his sweet potato bread as a demonstration. No one there could taste the difference between it and bread made with wheat flour. Later that year, Carver made his methods available to others in another bulletin, "How to Make Sweet Potato Flour, Starch, Sugar, Bread and Mock Cocoanut." It was reprinted in the *Literary Digest* and *Ladies' Home Journal.* By 1919, the government had two mills operating to make sweet potato flour.

The government was also interested in Carver's work with dehydrating vegetables. Dehydrated food was of special interest to the military because it was lightweight and easy to transport. One method that Carver used was what he called fruit leathers. He started by mashing overripe fruit to a pulp. He rolled that out like a piecrust and let it dry. Then he cut it into strips.

Carver did not discover food dehydration. The method he used for his fruit leathers dated back to the first century. It had been used in the days of Pompeii, an ancient city in Italy that was destroyed by a volcano in A.D. 79. Carver revived that method and introduced it to Americans.

Carver also experimented with creating dyes. Previously, the United States had imported dyes from Germany. That was no longer possible now that the United States was at war with Germany. The United States needed dyes to make camouflage clothes for the soldiers. No one knew how Germany made its dyes, but Carver worked on a method to make them from plants.

He was able to produce colors such as khaki, dark brown, and lemon from tomato vines. From the radish, he produced gray, black, and silver. He also created a variety of colors from dandelions, onions, sweet potatoes, peanuts, and the leaves and bark of maple and oak trees.

The war ended in late 1918, before the government could benefit from the dyes Carver created. But Carver continued with his work. In all, he was credited with creating more than five hundred dyes from twenty-eight kinds of plants.

After the war, interest in flour made from the sweet potato declined. Wheat flour was less expensive to produce, and there was no longer a wheat shortage. On the other hand, there was a shortage of drug crops, plants that could be used to produce medicines. The U.S. Department of Agriculture asked Carver to prepare a report on plants native to Macon County that could be used for medicine. Carver put together a list of one hundred fifteen plants. Then he published the list to encourage farmers to grow some of these plants on their farms as a way to increase their income.

Carver also continued his research into ways to use the peanut. In September 1920, the United Peanut Associations in Montgomery, Alabama, invited Carver to address their group.

Carver, carrying two heavy suitcases with his samples, arrived at the hotel in Montgomery where he was to speak. The doorman refused to let Carver enter. African Americans were not allowed. Carver finally convinced the doorman that he had been invited to speak at the hotel. Still he was not allowed to enter through the front door. The doorman sent Carver to the back of the hotel and told him he would have to use the freight elevator.

Carver took the freight elevator to the floor where the meeting was being held. Then he waited patiently while the members enjoyed their meal, a meal that Carver had not been invited to share because he was black.

Certainly, Carver saw the unfairness of such prejudice. He was respected for his knowledge. People wanted to hear what he had to say. In fact, members of the United Peanut Associations were quite impressed with his presentation that day. Because of that, they decided that they wanted Carver to represent them at the upcoming meeting of the Ways and Means Committee in Washington, D.C. But after his presentation, Carver closed up his cases, took the freight elevator down, and exited through the hotel's back door.

Carver chose not to talk about racial prejudice. Politics did not interest him. His religious beliefs and his work were his priorities. He felt that religion was the key to promoting understanding between races. "Real Christian people speak the same language," Carver once wrote. "They do unto others as they would have them do to them. The texture of the hair, nationality, and pigment of the skin has [sic] absolutely nothing to do with it."[6]

Although he did not discuss race, Carver would soon become an important figure in helping to promote understanding between the races.

Chapter 8

TALKS WITH "MR. CREATOR"

In 1923, two very different groups chose to honor Carver. One was the United Daughters of the Confederacy, a conservative white group. The other was the National Association for the Advancement of Colored People (NAACP), a prominent organization for civil rights. That year, the NAACP awarded Carver the Spingarn Medal for his research in agricultural chemistry. That annual award is given to the African-American person who has made the biggest contribution to the race during the previous year.

Shortly after receiving the Spingarn Medal, Carver was asked by the YMCA to speak at white colleges in the South. Carver spoke about science, but the real purpose of those speeches was to promote good will between races. An appearance at a regional summer conference in Blue Ridge, North Carolina, showed how well Carver handled that role. Delegates from several states attended the conference. As a form of protest, groups from Florida and Louisiana had planned to walk out during Carver's talk. That did not happen.

The delegates got so caught up in what Carver was saying that they forgot to leave. After Carver's presentation, the leader of the Florida delegation stood and announced to the group what they had intended to do. Then he apologized to Carver.

As Carver spoke at various colleges, he looked out over the audiences, observing the young men's faces. He was seeking those who seemed most interested in what he had to say. Later, he made a special effort to meet them. Carver became a mentor to these young men, whom he referred to as "my boys."[1] He kept in contact with them, taking an interest in their lives and writing them letters of encouragement. Some visited Carver at Tuskegee, and in some cases Carver developed friendships with their families, too.

Carver had a great influence on these young men's lives. Some went on to work for racial justice after they graduated from college. One urged the Texas Legislature to provide more money for education for African Americans. Another worked to improve working conditions for tenant farmers in Arkansas through an interracial organization called the Southern Tenant Farmers' Union. Several of Carver's "boys" became ministers, perhaps influenced by Carver's deep religious beliefs.

These young men and the Tuskegee students were Carver's family. Carver never married, and when he was asked why, he answered, "I never had time."[2]

According to reports, Carver once had a serious relationship with a young woman on the Tuskegee faculty. One of his friends later said that the cause of that breakup was that the woman was too concerned about the way Carver dressed.

"[Carver's] comment was that she was more interested in the way he dressed than the work he was doing," the friend explained.[3]

One of the things that set Carver apart from other scientists was his ability to join religion and science. Although some scientists rejected religion, Carver said that the inspiration for his scientific discoveries came from God. "The thing I am to do and the way of doing it comes to me. The method is revealed at the moment I am inspired to create something new. Without God to draw aside the curtain, I would be helpless," he once explained.[4]

Others did not share his point of view. In 1924, Carver was invited to speak to a women's group at the Marble Collegiate Church in New York City. During that presentation he spoke freely about his talks with "Mr. Creator," which led to his discoveries. He also mentioned that he never took books into his laboratory.

Two days later, an editorial appeared in The New York Times criticizing Carver's methods. "Real chemists, or at any rate other real chemists, do not scorn books out of which they can learn what other chemists have done, and they do not ascribe their successes, when they have any, to 'inspiration,'" the editor wrote.[5]

Carver was upset by the editorial because he felt that he had been misunderstood. Certainly he did not discourage anyone from using books. He wrote a reply to the editor noting that he had a good education including a master's degree from Iowa State College. He said that he received the leading scientific publications and had been influenced by a great number of scientists. He kept books written by these scientists in his own library.

The reason he did not take books into his laboratory was that much of the work he did had not been done before. Then he gave an example of what he meant. He said that while he was in New York, he had noticed the edible roots of two kinds of plants—taros and yautias—that were on display in grocery markets. It got him thinking about the products that could be developed from these roots. "I know of no one who has ever worked with these roots in this way," Carver wrote. "I know of no book from which I can get this information, yet I will have no trouble in doing it."[6] The New York Times never printed Carver's letter. But Carver's friends sent copies to other newspapers, which did print it.

Another thing that Carver said during his speech at the Marble Collegiate Church was that he had never profited from his discoveries. "Somebody who had benefited by one of my products from the peanut sent me $100 the other day, but I sent it back to him," he noted.[7] It was something he had repeated often in his career.

Carver received a huge volume of mail. Some of the letters were invitations for him to give a speech or make an appearance. There were also requests for his bulletins and personal letters from friends and former students. Other letters were from people asking his advice on a particular problem. Many of these writers sent a few dollars as payment. Carver gave his advice, but he always returned the money.

By 1923, Carver was also receiving letters from people all over the United States who were interested in manufacturing his products. It was an opportunity to help southern farmers by opening new markets for their crops. But Carver was a creator, not a businessman. He did not want to get involved in the day-to-day work of manufacturing.

Carver hired Ernest Thompson, a young white man, to act as his business manager. It would be Thompson's job to investigate new opportunities for manufacturing Carver's products. In March 1923, Thompson arranged for an exhibit of Carver's products on the roof of the Hotel Cecil in Atlanta, Georgia. That exhibit and the publicity it got led to the formation of a company known as the Carver Products Company. It was organized by a group of Atlanta businessmen. Carver's role was to serve as consulting chemist and research engineer.

Organizers decided that Carver's paints and stains would be the easiest products to get up and running, so they focused on them first. In a letter dated May 22, 1924, Carver said that plans were finalized for a paint plant to be built in the Tuskegee area. They also applied for patents. In 1926, Carver was issued a patent for a paint and stain process that he had developed, and in 1927, he was given another patent for a paint process. He also received a patent for a cosmetic product. Unfortunately, the company never really got off the ground, and it went out of business after four years.

Thompson and several Tuskegee businessmen started another company, called the Carver Penol Company, sometime around 1925. They manufactured Penol, a mixture of creosote and peanuts. Creosote is a liquid made from wood tar. It was used as the base of a medicine to treat respiratory illnesses. The medicine tasted bad and often caused nausea. Carver's idea was to add peanuts to the mixture to make it taste better and to give it some nutritional value. Like the Carver Products Company, the Carver Penol Company enjoyed little success.

Although Carver's attempts at manufacturing his products did not work out, other manufacturers sought his advice. He also continued to be a spokesperson for the peanut industry.

During his lifetime, Carver created more than three hundred products from peanuts, though history has shown that he was not the first to come up with some of his uses for the peanut. In 1885, B. W. Jones had published a report titled The Peanut Plant. That report told how coffee, chocolate, and bread could be made from peanuts. Carver has been credited with the discovery of peanut butter, but other reports show that an unknown St. Louis physician made that discovery in 1890. Peanuts: Culture and Uses, a government publication released in 1895, noted several uses of the peanut, including making margarine and soap. Most of Carver's work with peanuts was done after 1903. Still, even though others experimented with uses for the peanut, Carver did the most to promote it. He continued in that role, giving many presentations.

Carver also urged people to make use of whatever was available to them. In the fall of 1927, he gave a speech in Tulsa, Oklahoma. In the early morning hours before his presentation, he took a walk on nearby Stand Pipe Hill. During his excursion, he gathered twenty-seven plants that could be used in making medicine. Then he went to a local drugstore. "I found down in

Ferguson's Drug Store on North Greenwood, seven patent medicines containing in their formulas certain elements contained in these plants on Stand Pipe Hill," Carver said.[8] He noted that the medicines had been shipped in from New York, but they could have been manufactured locally.

In 1928, Carver was invited to speak in Albany, Georgia, on behalf of the Pecan Exchange. In his laboratory, he had also worked on finding uses for the pecan, creating seventy-five products.

That same year, Simpson College awarded Carver an honorary doctor of science degree. The doctorate, or Ph.D., is the highest degree given by a college or university. People who earn it are called doctor. However, Carver had been called Dr. Carver for years already. In a letter to his friend Dr. Pammel, Carver explained how that came about.

It was started by Daniel Smith, an accountant from New York who traveled to Tuskegee each year to audit the institute's accounts. Smith was always very interested in Carver's work. One time, he asked if Carver had a doctoral degree. When Carver said no, Smith said that he should have, that his work entitled him to it. From that time on, Smith called him Dr. Carver. Smith also wrote articles in which he referred to him as Dr. Carver. Soon others began to call him Dr., too. Carver appeared almost embarrassed about the misuse of that title. "I regret that such an appendage was tacked on but I cannot help it," he wrote.[9]

He no longer needed to feel embarrassed. The honor from Simpson College meant that he was worthy of the title. Unfortunately, Carver was not able to attend the ceremonies at the college. A few days before the presentation, he was attacked by a bull at the institute. His injuries were not serious, but they did keep him from making the trip to Iowa.

In October 1929, the stock market crashed, marking the start of the Great Depression. It was the biggest economic crisis the United States had ever experienced. People lost their jobs and banks closed. Soup lines became a familiar sight as people could not afford to buy food.

Money was not important to Carver. There were stories around campus that he would stash his checks in a drawer, forgetting to take them to the bank. Occasionally, the institute's bookkeeper would remind Carver to cash his checks.

Although Carver was careless about his paychecks, he did have accounts in two local banks. He also still had an account in a bank in Iowa. During the Depression, his savings were frozen when all three banks crashed. It meant that Carver's money was not available to him, but he was not upset. "I guess somebody found a use for the money," he said. "I wasn't using it."[10] Carver was later able to recover some of his losses.

Carver's message about making do with what was available became even more important during the Depression, when people had to get by with what little they had. Carver talked about how to eat healthy foods on a limited budget, and he wrote articles that included recipes using ingredients that families could grow in their gardens.

In 1930, the price of cotton dropped to an all-time low. In his laboratory, Carver worked to find new uses for cotton to increase the demand for it. One idea that he worked on was cotton paving blocks to be used in road building. People in other states were also doing similar experiments, but Carver continued to conduct his own research. Eventually, he created seventeen paving products using cotton.

By 1930, there were so many requests for Carver to make personal appearances that the institute decided he needed a traveling secretary. Harry O. Abbott was hired to make all of Carver's travel arrangements and to travel with him. Carver's schedule would soon be even more demanding.

Chapter 9

BECOMING A
TRAILBLAZER

B y the 1930s, Carver had begun experimenting with peanut-oil massages as a way to restore withered muscles. He got the idea after creating a face cream that had a peanut-oil base. Some of the women who tried it returned it to Carver complaining that the cream made their faces fat. Carver thought that if the cream could nourish the healthy facial muscles of these women, it might also bring life back to damaged muscles. He put that theory to work with good results.

On December 30, 1933, the Associated Press, a national news network, published a story about two young men Carver had helped with peanut-oil massages. One had been kicked in the kneecap by a horse. The accident tore the ligaments surrounding his knee. As they healed, they tightened up until that leg was six inches shorter than the other one. Carver began daily massages with peanut oil. Within six weeks, the young man was able to walk with only a slight limp. Within a year, he was walking normally. He went on to become a pitcher on his college baseball team.

The other case was a boy whose leg had been withered by polio. This infectious disease attacked thousands of people, especially the young. In some cases, the disease was mild. Other times, it attacked the central nervous system, leading to paralysis and sometimes death. Under Carver's care, the young man gradually went from using crutches to walking with a cane. His recovery was so complete that he was eventually able to play football.

After the Associated Press article was published, rumors spread that Carver had discovered a cure for polio. It was a claim that he quickly denied. In fact, Carver did not treat any patients until after they had recovered from the disease. Then he went to work restoring muscles that had been left useless. Once people found out about Carver's work, they flocked to the Tuskegee campus seeking treatment for themselves or their children.

During 1934, most of Carver's weekends were spent massaging polio victims. Patients came once a week for treatment, but Carver also trained a friend or relative of the patient to give daily massages. Carver refused payment for his work, but some patients, wanting to show their appreciation, made donations to the institute.

Many people showed remarkable improvements under Carver's care. Carver believed that the combination of peanut oil and massage was the reason for these improvements. Medical experts did not believe that the peanut oil helped.

They said that it was Carver's massage techniques that restored life to the muscles. Carver continued his work with peanut oil massages throughout much of the 1930s. It was not until 1954 that Dr. Jonas Salk discovered a polio vaccine.

In 1935, Carver was appointed a collaborator with the U.S. Department of Agriculture in a plant disease survey. Since his graduation from Iowa State College, Carver had not had much time to pursue his interest in mycology. This new appointment gave him an opportunity to return to the study of fungi and plant diseases.

That year Carver also got unexpected help when Austin W. Curtis, Jr., was hired as his laboratory assistant. Curtis was a graduate of Cornell University with a bachelor's degree in chemistry. Carver had had laboratory assistants in the past, but he was used to working alone. He had trouble delegating work to others. As a result, his assistants did not have much to do. They quickly moved on to other jobs.

Curtis's first meeting with Carver was not encouraging. When Curtis arrived on campus, a Mr. Williston took him to meet Carver. "We proceeded to Dr. Carver's apartment, which was in Rockefeller Hall," Curtis recalled. "Mr. Williston knocked on the door and after what seemed like an eternity, the door opened, just probably six or eight inches and Dr. Carver said 'Yes?' and Mr. Williston said, 'Carver, here's Curtis who is to be your assistant.' And Dr. Carver said, 'How do you do and good night.'"[1] Then he closed the door.

The next morning, Carver met briefly with Curtis. He told Curtis to get acquainted with the institute and then sent him on his way. Those short daily meetings became a routine, but it would be a while before Curtis understood his role as Carver's assistant.

Curtis had been at the institute for six weeks before Carver finally gave him an assignment. In the meantime, Curtis worked on his own projects in the laboratory. "Each morning I had to come into his office and he would only ask questions as to what I had done during the previous day," Curtis said.[2]

Curtis also learned early on that Carver expected everything to be exact. He had been at the institute just two or three days when he took a telephone message for Carver. When Carver saw the message, he scolded Curtis for forgetting to include the date. The message was not important, but Curtis understood Carver's point. "His reason was sound," Curtis explained. "If you get in the habit of putting the date on everything, it will always be on important things."[3]

Carver gradually accepted his young assistant and grew to treat him like a son. They enjoyed a successful working relationship that lasted until Carver died.

By 1935, a new science called chemurgy was emerging. The purpose of this science was to find industrial uses for farm products. Today, this science is called biochemical engineering. It was the kind of work that Carver had been doing for some time. In fact, some have called him the father of chemurgy.[4]

In 1935, a group of farm leaders, scientists, and manufacturers met in Dearborn, Michigan, to discuss how agricultural products could be used in industry. The result of that meeting was the founding of the National Farm Chemurgic Council. Carver was invited to speak at the first Chemurgic Conference. He was not able to attend that conference, but in 1937 he was invited to speak again at another conference in Dearborn. This time he accepted.

Henry Ford, founder of the Ford Motor Company, was also investigating this new science. He already had researchers working on ways to use soybeans in industry. The two men met at the conference. With their common interest in this new science, they quickly became friends, and Ford later visited Carver at Tuskegee.

After the Chemurgic Conference, Carver returned to Tuskegee to celebrate his fortieth anniversary at the institute. A bronze bust of Carver, sculpted by Steffen Wolfgang George Thomas of Atlanta, Georgia, was unveiled during commencement ceremonies on June 2, 1937. Carver's friends and admirers had paid for the sculpture with one-dollar donations. Carver appeared at the ceremony wearing the same suit he had worn for his graduation from Iowa State College more than forty years earlier.

By that time, Carver's fame had spread far beyond the Tuskegee campus. In 1937, he was invited to be a guest on several national radio programs. In addition, the Smithsonian Institution in Washington, D.C., produced a series of radio shows about Carver's life. The shows were broadcast nationwide. Schools all across the United States were named for him. In fact, there were so many schools named after him in Alabama that in 1938 Carver suggested that one school choose a different name. Other African-American facilities were also named for him, including a swimming pool, a theater, and an office building.

In 1938, a movie titled *The Life of George Washington Carver* was released. It was made in Hollywood by the Pete Smith Specialty Company. An actor played the role of Carver as a young man in the film, but Carver played himself as an older man.

Unfortunately, failing health forced Carver to cut back on some of his traveling in 1938. He suffered from pernicious anemia, an inability to absorb vitamin B_{12}. He spent much of that year in the hospital. At that time Carver began seeking ways that his work would be remembered and continued. It led to the founding of the George Washington Carver Museum, which Carver hoped would preserve his memory and serve as an inspiration to future scientists.

The institute donated an old laundry building to be used for the museum. When Carver was released from the hospital, he moved into living quarters in Dorothy Hall. It made it more convenient for him to work on the museum, which was located next door. The museum opened in 1939, although it was not yet finished.

That year, Carver was awarded the Roosevelt Memorial Award for his contributions to southern agriculture. He was also elected an honorary member of the American Inventors Society.

In 1940, Carver donated much of his life savings to establish the George Washington Carver Foundation, which provided for a research center. Carver hoped that through the foundation his work would live on and others would build on it. "I am only a trail blazer for those who came after me," he said. "I hope the South will be the first to take advantage of the foundation and contribute to it. And I hope the foundation will serve all the people, regardless of race, color or creed."[5]

In March 1941, Mr. and Mrs. Henry Ford traveled to Tuskegee to officially dedicate the George Washington Carver Museum. The museum contained Carver's collections of plant and mineral specimens; products made from peanuts, sweet potatoes, and clays; equipment from his first laboratory; and his paintings. It also included an exhibit of his needlework.

Ford saw how difficult it was for Carver to climb the nineteen steps to his room, and later had an elevator installed in Dorothy Hall. Although Carver was frail, he had not lost his sense of humor. A reporter who attended the dedication at the museum referred to Carver in his article as "toothless."[6] Carver, who had never adjusted to wearing dentures, did not agree. "If he had taken the trouble to inquire I could have proved I am not toothless," he said. "I had my teeth right in my pocket all the time."[7]

On December 7, 1941, the Japanese bombed the U.S. naval base at Pearl Harbor, bringing the United States into World War II. Once again there was a worldwide food shortage, just as there had been during World War I. Carver's suggestions for preserving food and for food substitutions were still as vital as they had been more than twenty years earlier.

The government urged people to plant gardens, called Victory Gardens. In keeping with that message, Carver published a bulletin in 1942 titled "Nature's Garden for Victory and Peace." The bulletin listed more than a hundred grasses, weeds, and wildflowers that could be used for food. It also included recipes.

In July 1942, Carver traveled to Dearborn, Michigan, the home of his friend Henry Ford. Ford had built a replica of the log cabin where Carver had lived as a child and a nutritional laboratory to honor Carver and his achievements. The log cabin was displayed in Greenfield Village located next to the Henry Ford Museum in Dearborn. Greenfield Village, founded by Henry Ford in 1929, is a collection of historical homes and buildings. Carver spent several weeks in Dearborn, returning to Tuskegee in August.

He continued working, but he was obviously weak. One day in December he fell as he was entering the Carver Museum. He never fully recovered from that fall. On January 5, 1943, he lay down for a nap and never woke up. He was buried on the Tuskegee Institute campus near the grave of Booker T. Washington.

Chapter 10

ONGOING FAME

On February 5, 1943, Representative Dewey Short and Senator Harry S. Truman introduced bills in Congress to make Carver's birthplace in Diamond, Missouri, a national monument. President Franklin D. Roosevelt signed that legislation on July 14, 1943. Carver was only the third person to receive such an honor. The other two were George Washington and Abraham Lincoln.

Today, the 210-acre park includes a museum with exhibits highlighting events in Carver's life. There is also a walking trail where visitors can experience the woods and prairie areas that Carver once enjoyed.

There have been many honors for Carver since his death. The United States government has issued two postage stamps with Carver's picture on them, and there have been two ships named for him. His image was also imprinted on a fifty-cent coin. In 1956, Simpson College dedicated a new science building to Carver, and Iowa State University did the same in 1970.

In 1976, Carver was enshrined in the Hall of Fame for Great Americans in New York City. He was only the second African American to receive that honor. The first was Booker T. Washington.

The Hall of Fame ceremony was held at the Tuskegee Institute. More than fifteen hundred people crowded into the school's chapel, where a bronze bust of Carver was unveiled. Richmond Barthe, a prominent African-American artist, sculpted the bust.

Dr. John Hope Franklin, a noted historian, was the keynote speaker at the ceremony. He talked about the way Carver's life had changed direction when he arrived in Tuskegee. "If George Washington Carver had not been driven by the strongly felt need to formulate programs of scientific agriculture that would raise the living standard for Black farmers in the South," Franklin said, "he may well have been the country's leading mycologist. Some of the best work in that field was done by Carver as he worked toward his master's degree at Iowa State College; and his early papers on plant fungi clearly established him as a leader in that important field."[1]

Others believe that Carver might also have established himself as a great artist, but he chose a different path. The decisions Carver made regarding the direction of his career are most eloquently described on his gravestone: "He could have added fortune to fame, but caring for neither, he found happiness and honor in being helpful to the world."[2]

In 1990, more than forty-five years after his death, Carver received yet another honor. That year, Carver and Percy Julian became the first African Americans inducted into the National

Inventors Hall of Fame (NIHF). A requirement for induction into that institution is that members have a patent on an invention. In his lifetime, Carver had applied for only three patents. It was enough for induction into the Hall of Fame, but it was not a good representation of Carver's accomplishments. That was noted by attorney Allen Jensen, president of the NIHF foundation. "Carver was inducted as much for his dedication and service to mankind as for his inventions," Jensen explained.[3]

Carver helped thousands of southern farmers improve their lives by steering them away from a one-crop system. As a scientist he was a leader in finding industrial uses for agricultural products. Because of the fame he achieved in that role, he opened doors for other African-American scientists who followed. Perhaps his greatest legacy is the individual lives he touched as a teacher and a mentor, the young people he guided and inspired.

"When you do the common things of life in an uncommon way," Carver told his students, "you will command the attention of the world."[4] George Washington Carver did just that.

CHRONOLOGY

1864?—Born on the Moses Carver farm in Diamond, Missouri.

1878—Earns certificate of merit from one-room schoolhouse in Neosho, Missouri.

1884—Ends his high school studies in Minneapolis, Kansas.

1886—Becomes a homesteader, settling near Beeler, Kansas.

1890—Enrolls at Simpson College in Indianola, Iowa.

1891—Transfers to the Iowa State College of Agriculture and Mechanical Arts, now called Iowa State University, in Ames, Iowa.

1894—Earns a bachelor of science degree in agriculture from Iowa State College of Agriculture and Mechanical Arts.

1896—Earns a master's of agriculture degree from Iowa State College of Agriculture and Mechanical Arts; accepts a position as head of a new agricultural department at the Tuskegee Institute in Tuskegee, Alabama.

1906—Starts Jesup Wagon, a movable school to reach farmers.

1910—Introduces a new cotton hybrid officially named Carver's Hybrid.

1916—Becomes a fellow of England's Royal Society of Arts, Manufacturers and Commerce.

1918—Is invited to Washington, D.C., to discuss his method of making flour from sweet potatoes.

1921—Appears before the Ways and Means Committee of the U.S. House of Representatives.

1923—Receives the Spingarn Medal from the National Association for the Advancement of Colored People (NAACP) for distinguished service to science; is also honored by the United Daughters of the Confederacy.

1928—Receives an honorary doctor of science degree from Simpson College.

1935—Is appointed a collaborator with the U.S. Department of Agriculture in a plant disease survey.

1937—Celebrates his fortieth anniversary at the Tuskegee Institute.

1939—Receives the Roosevelt Medal and is elected an honorary member in the American Inventors Society. George Washington Carver Museum opens.

1940—Establishes the George Washington Carver Foundation for research.

1941—Mr. and Mrs. Henry Ford dedicate the George Washington Carver Museum on the Tuskegee campus.

1943—Dies on January 5 and is buried on the Tuskegee Institute campus; President Franklin D. Roosevelt signs legislation to make Carver's birthplace a national monument.

1976—Is enshrined in the Hall of Fame for Great Americans in New York City.

1990—Is inducted into the National Inventors Hall of Fame.

SELECTED RECIPES BY DR. CARVER

These are historical recipes. The publisher has not tested them. Be sure to ask an adult for help before trying any of these recipes.

SWEET POTATO RECIPES

From George Washington Carver, "How the Farmer Can Save His Sweet Potatoes and Ways of Preparing Them for the Table." Tuskegee Institute, Fourth Edition, 1937.

Sweet Potatoes Baked with Apples

Take four medium sized potatoes and the same number of apples. Wash, peel and cut the potatoes in slices about ¼ of an inch thick; pare and slice the apples in the same way; put in baking dish in alternate layers; sprinkle 1½ cups of sugar over the top, scatter ½ cup of butter also over the top; add ¾ pint of hot water; bake slowly for one hour; serve steaming hot.

Sweet Potato Muffins

Boil until thoroughly done a sweet potato weighing about ¾ of a pound; mash very fine; pass through colander to free it from lumps; add to it a large tablespoonful of butter and a little salt; whip well, now add ½ cupful of milk and two well-beaten eggs and flour enough to make a soft batter, which will be about two cupfuls. Before adding the flour, sift into it one teaspoon of baking powder. Bake in muffin rings or gem pans.

A Southern Dish

Cut cold baked sweet potatoes into slices and put into an earthen dish; add sugar and butter to each layer and bake until slightly brown.

Sweet Potato Pie

Boil potatoes in skins. When tender, remove skins; mash and beat until light. To each pint of potatoes, add ½ pint of milk, ½ pint of cream, and four well-beaten eggs; add 1½ teacups of sugar (less if the potatoes are very sweet). Add spice, cinnamon, and ginger to taste; one ground clove will improve it. Bake with bottom crust only. The above is enough to make five or six pies.

Delicious Potatoes

Wash and pare rather small sized potatoes; steam or boil until they can be readily pierced with a fork; dry the surplus water off; have a little butter melted in a dish, roll the potatoes in this; place in a quick oven and brown slightly; serve hot.

PEANUT RECIPES

From George Washington Carver, "How to Grow the Peanut and 105 Ways of Preparing It for Human Consumption." Tuskegee Institute, Fourth Edition, 1925.

Peanut Candy

2 cups sugar, ½ cup milk, 2 tablespoons peanut butter. Blend together; boil for 5 minutes; remove from the fire and beat steadily till cool.

Peanut Butter Fudge

2 cups powdered sugar, 1 cup milk, 2 heaping teaspoons peanut butter. Mix ingredients; boil vigorously for 5 minutes; beat; pour in a buttered pan, and cut in squares.

Peanut Brownies

2 eggs, 2 squares chocolate, 1 cup sugar, ½ cup flour, ½ cup melted butter, $1/8$ cup coarsely ground peanuts.

Mix and bake in shallow pan in a quick oven; garnish the top with nuts, cut in squares.

Peanut and Date Salad

2 cups dates, stoned and cut into small pieces, ½ cup coarsely ground peanuts, 2 cups celery, finely cut. Stir well, then mix with cream salad dressing.

Peanut Bisque

To 3 cups of boiling milk, add half a teaspoon chopped onion, a pinch of salt and pepper; rub to a smooth paste a tablespoon of flour with water; add half cup of peanut butter; stir in the flour; boil 3 minutes longer; serve with peanut wafers (recipe follows).

Peanut Wafers

2 cups flour, 1 cup water, 1 cup powdered sugar, ½ cup rolled peanuts, ½ cup butter. Rub the butter and sugar together until light and creamy; add the flour and water alternately. Lastly add the peanuts; drop on buttered tins, and bake quickly. Cut into squares while hot, as it soon gets brittle after baking.

CHAPTER NOTES

Chapter 1. "The Peanut Man"

1. Medora Field Perkerson, "Southern Slave Becomes Great Scientist," *Atlanta Journal*, March 18, 1923, p. 1.

2. Ibid.

3. *Tariff Information, 1921. Hearings Before the Committee on Ways and Means House of Representatives on Schedule G Agricultural Products and Provisions, January 21, 1921.* Washington, D.C.: Government Printing Office, 1921, p. 1543.

4. Ibid., p. 1544.

5. Ibid.

6. "Dr. Carver Is Dead; Negro Scientist," *The New York Times*, January 6, 1943, p. 25.

7. *Tariff Information*, 1921, p. 1545.

8. "Peanut Man," *Time*, June 14, 1939, p. 54.

Chapter 2. "The Plant Doctor"

1. George Washington Carver, untitled autobiographical sketch, ca. 1922, George Washington Carver Papers, Tuskegee Institute Archives on microfilm, Reel 1.

2. George Washington Carver, untitled autobiographical sketch, ca. 1897, George Washington Carver Papers, Tuskegee Institute Archives on microfilm, Reel 1.

3. Ibid.

4. Ibid.

5. Medora Field Perkerson, "Southern Slave Becomes Great Scientist," *Atlanta Journal*, March 18, 1923, p. 1.

6. Robert P. Fuller and Merrill J. Mattes, *The Early Life of George Washington Carver*, unpublished manuscript, 1957, available at the George Washington Carver National Monument Archives, p. 47.

Chapter 3. In Search of an Education

1. Robert P. Fuller and Merrill J. Mattes, *The Early Life of George Washington Carver*, unpublished manuscript, 1957, available at the George Washington Carver National Monument Archives, p. 51.

2. Ibid., p. 64.

3. George Washington Carver, untitled autobiographical sketch, ca. 1922, George Washington Carver Papers, Tuskegee Institute Archives on microfilm, Reel 1.

4. Letter from George Washington Carver to Dr. L. H. Pammel, dated May 5, 1922, on file at the Iowa State University Archives, Box 1, File 16.

5. Linda O. McMurry, *George Washington Carver: Scientist and Symbol*, New York: Oxford University Press, 1981, p. 24.

6. E. C. Ford, "A Visit With George Washington Carver," *The Negro History Bulletin*, October 1953, p. 5.

7. Edwin R. Embree, *13 Against the Odds*, Port Washington, N.Y.: Kennikat Press, Inc., 1944, p. 103.

8. George Washington Carver, untitled autobiographical sketch, ca. 1897, George Washington Carver Papers, Tuskegee Institute Archives on microfilm, Reel 1.

9. McMurry, p. 29.

Chapter 4. "Cast Down Your Bucket Where You Are"

1. Lulu Mae Coe, "Washington Carver as a Struggling Student," *Des Moines Sunday Register*, January 17, 1943, Iowa News, p. 5.

2. "Black Leonardo," *Time*, November 24, 1941, p. 81.

3. Letter from George Washington Carver to Dr. L. H. Pammel, dated May 5, 1922, on file at the Iowa State University Archives, Box 1, File 16.

4. Letter from George Washington Carver to Dr. L. H. Pammel, dated April 29, 1918, on file at the Iowa State University Archives, Box 1, File 16.

5. Linda O. McMurry, *George Washington Carver: Scientist and Symbol*, New York: Oxford University Press, 1981, p. 41.

6. "Goober Wizard: Negro Scientist Turns Peanuts into Vital Crop for Dixie Farmers," *Literary Digest*, June 12, 1937, p. 21.

7. Emma Lou Thornbrough, ed., *Booker T. Washington*, Englewood Cliffs, N.J.: Prentice-Hall, Inc., 1969, p. 34.

8. Letter from George Washington Carver to Booker T. Washington, dated April 12, 1896, George Washington Carver Papers, Tuskegee Institute Archives on microfilm, Reel 1.

Chapter 5. Scientific Agriculture

1. Stanley High, "Dr. Carver Wanted No Greener Pastures," *Baltimore Sun*, November 8, 1942.

2. Mildred Sandison Fenner, "George Washington Carver— The Wizard of Tuskegee," *NEA Journal*, December, 1946, p. 581.

3. Ibid.

4. Booker T. Washington, *My Larger Education*, excerpt reprinted in *The Alumnus*, published by Iowa State University, February 1913, p. 6.

5. James Saxon Childers, "A Boy Who Was Traded for a Horse," *Reader's Digest*, February 1937, p. 8.

6. Washington, p. 6.

7. Letter from George Washington Carver to Mrs. L. H. Pammel, dated March 30, 1897, on file at the Iowa State University Archives, Box 1, File 15.

8. Letter from George Washington Carver to members of the Tuskegee Finance Committee, dated November 27, 1896, George Washington Carver Papers, Tuskegee Institute Archives on microfilm, Reel 1.

9. "Colored Alumnus Is Doing a Great Work," *Ames Evening Times*, June 11, 1921.

10. Peter H. Martorella, "The Negro's Role in American History: George Washington Carver—A Case Study," *The Social Studies*, December 1969, p. 320.

Chapter 6. Reaching Out to Farmers and Students

1. Letter from George Washington Carver to Booker T. Washington, dated November 28, 1902, George Washington Carver Papers, Tuskegee Institute Archives on microfilm, Reel 2.

2. Letter from George Washington Carver to Booker T. Washington, dated October 14, 1904, George Washington Carver Papers, Tuskegee Institute Archives on microfilm, Reel 2.

3. Stanley High, "Dr. Carver Wanted No Greener Pastures," *Baltimore Sun*, November 8, 1942.

Chapter 7. The Boll Weevil, War, and Racial Prejudice

1. "Peanuts: How Scientist's 145 Varieties Helped Lowly 'Goober' to Rise," *Popular Science Monthly*, p. 68.

2. W. W. Wheeler, "'Great Creator,' I said. '*Why* Did You Make the Peanut?'" *Farm and Fireside*, November 1928, p. 8.

3. Letter from George Washington Carver to Mr. Scott, dated February 15, 1916, George Washington Carver Papers, Tuskegee Institute Archives on microfilm, Reel 5.

4. Wheeler, p. 32.

5. Ibid.

6. Linda O. Hines, "White Mythology and Black Duality: George W. Carver's Response to Racism and the Radical Left," *Journal of Negro History*, April 1977, p. 135.

Chapter 8. Talks with "Mr. Creator"

1. Display in the museum at the George Washington Carver National Monument in Diamond, Missouri.

2. Mildred Sandison Fenner, "George Washington Carver— The Wizard of Tuskegee," *NEA Journal*, December 1946, p. 581.

3. Toby Fishbein, transcript of oral interview with Austin W. Curtis, Detroit, Michigan, March 3, 1979, on file at the Iowa State University Archives, Box 1, File 8.

4. Josephine C. Walker, "George Washington Carver: Scientist and Saint," *Sepia*, August 1980, p. 19.

5. "Men of Science Never Talk That Way," *The New York Times*, November 20, 1924.

6. Letter from George Washington Carver to the editor of *The New York Times*, dated November 24, 1924, on file at the Iowa State University Archives, Box 1, File 18.

7. "Negro's Chemistry Astounds Audience," *The New York Times*, November 19, 1924.

8. "Finds Rubber Forest in Tulsa," *Black Dispatch*, Oklahoma City, Okla., October 13, 1927.

9. Letter from George Washington Carver to Dr. L. H. Pammel, dated November 26, 1926, on file at the Iowa State University Archives, Box 1, File 17.

10. Rackham Holt, *George Washington Carver*, Garden City, N.Y.: Doubleday & Company, Inc., 1943, p. 301.

Chapter 9. Becoming a Trailblazer

1. Toby Fishbein, transcript of oral interview with Austin W. Curtis, Detroit, Michigan, March 3, 1979, on file at the Iowa State University Archives, Box 1, File 8, pp. 1–2.

2. Ibid.

3. John Askins, "Biography News," *Detroit Free Press*, May/June 1975, p. 511.

4. Brochure from the George Washington Carver Museum, on file at the Iowa State University Archives, Box 2, File 3.

5. "Dr. Carver, Peanut Wizard, Dies at 79," *Washington Daily News*, January 6, 1943.

6. "Black Leonardo," *Time*, November 24, 1941, p. 82.

7. Rackham Holt, *George Washington Carver*, Garden City, N.Y.: Doubleday & Company, Inc., 1943, p. 328.

Chapter 10. Ongoing Fame

1. "Another Honor for the 'Peanut' Man: Botanist George Washington Carver Is Named to the Hall of Fame for Great Americans," *Ebony*, July 1977, p. 103.

2. Samuel P. Massie, "The George Washington Carver Story," *Chemistry*, September 1970, p. 21.

3. Joan Morgan, "Joining the Ranks of Invention Heroes: Dr. George Washington Carver & Dr. Percy Julian," *Black Issues in Higher Education*, May 10, 1990, p. 10.

4. James Saxon Childers, "A Boy Who Was Traded for a Horse," *Reader's Digest*, February 1937, p. 6.

FURTHER READING

Burgan, Michael. *George Washington Carver: Scientist, Inventor, and Teacher*. Mankato, Minn.: Compass Point Books, 2007.

Halvorsen, Lisa. *George Washington Carver*. Farmington Hills, Minn.: Blackbirch Press, 2002.

Kremer, Gary R., editor. *George Washington Carver: A Biography*. Santa Barbara, Calif.: ABC-CLIO, Inc., 2011.

Schier, Helga. *George Washington Carver: Agricultural Innovator*. Edina, Minn.: Abdo Publishing Company, 2008.

Tarrant-Reid, Linda. *Discovering Black America: From the Age of Exploration to the Twenty-First Century*. New York: Abrams Books, 2012.

Wheeler, Jill C. *George Washington Carver*. Minneapolis, Minn.: Abdo Publishing Company, 2003.

INDEX